RANJOT SINGH CHAHAL

How to Make an Amazing Trip Around the World

Rana Books

First published by Rana Books (UK, INDIA) 2023

First edition

ISBN: 978-81-19786-57-2

Contents

Chapter 1: Selecting Your Destinations

1.1 Researching Potential Countries

When planning a trip one of the first steps is to research potential countries that you may want to visit. This involves gathering information about different destinations and determining which ones align with your interests and preferences. Here are some key factors to consider during this process:

- Safety and Security: It is important to prioritize your safety when choosing a destination. Research the current political climate crime rates and any travel advisories issued by your government. Explore forums and travel websites to read about other travelers' experiences in the country.

- Visa Requirements: Check the visa requirements for each country you are considering. Some countries offer visa-free entry while others require visas that may involve a complex application process. Make sure you have ample time to obtain any necessary visas.

- Weather and Seasons: Consider the climate and seasons of the countries you are interested in. Some countries may be best to visit during a particular time of year while others may have more favorable weather conditions for your preferred activities.

- Cultural Differences: Research the cultural norms customs and etiquette of the countries you are considering. It is essential to have an understanding of local traditions and respect them to ensure a positive travel experience.

1.2 Considering Your Interests and Budget

Once you have narrowed down your list of potential countries it is important to consider your interests and budget. While traveling you'll want to engage in activities and experiences that align with your preferences. Here are some factors to consider:

- Interests: Think about the activities and experiences you enjoy the most such as historical sites adventure sports beaches wildlife art culture or cuisine. Consider the countries that offer the most opportunities for your preferred activities.

- Budget: Take into account your financial capabilities. Determine how much you're willing to spend on accommodation meals transportation activities and souvenirs. Some countries may be more affordable to visit than others considering factors like the cost of living and exchange rates.

- Transportation: Look into transportation options within the countries you are considering. Consider the availability cost and convenience of flights trains buses and other modes of transportation. Distance and ease of travel between different destinations within a country can greatly impact your itinerary.

- Accommodation: Research the availability and cost of accommodation options such as hotels hostels guesthouses or vacation rentals in the countries you are considering. Consider your preferred level of comfort and the proximity of accommodations to desired attractions.

1.3 Determining the Length of Your Trip

The length of your trip can greatly impact the destinations you choose to visit. It is important to determine the duration of your journey before finalizing your itinerary. Here are some factors to consider:

- Time Constraints: Assess how much time you can allocate to your trip. This will depend on various factors such as work or school schedules personal commitments and financial considerations. Determine if you have a fixed number of vacation days or if you have the freedom to plan an extended trip.

- Prioritizing Destinations: Consider the number of countries you want to visit and the time you are willing to spend in each. Some destinations may require more time to fully explore while others can be covered in a shorter duration. Prioritize your must-visit places and allocate time accordingly.

- Travel Pace: Determine your preferred travel pace. Some people prefer a relaxed trip spending more time in each location to fully immerse themselves in the local culture. Others prefer a faster pace trying to see as many places as possible. Consider your personal preferences and energy levels.

- Travel Logistics: Consider the time required for transportation between destinations. Some countries may have limited transportation options which could increase travel time. Factor in transit times especially if you plan to visit multiple countries.

Example:

Let's say you are planning a trip to Southeast Asia. After researching potential countries and considering your interests and budget you have narrowed down your choices to Thailand Vietnam and Cambodia.

- Safety and Security: You check the travel advisories and find that all three countries are generally safe for travelers. However you make a note to avoid certain areas that may have higher crime rates.

- Visa Requirements: Thailand offers visa-free entry for most nationalities while Vietnam and Cambodia require visas. You decide to allocate time for visa applications and choose countries that offer visa-on-arrival options.

- Weather and Seasons: You discover that Thailand has a tropical climate with hot and humid weather year-round. Vietnam experiences distinct seasons with the north being cooler in winter. Cambodia has a similar climate to Thailand. Based on your preference for warm weather you prioritize Thailand during the winter months.

- Cultural Differences: You research the cultural norms of each country and find that Buddhism heavily influences the culture in Thailand and Cambodia while Vietnamese culture has influences from Confucianism. You make a note to dress modestly and respect local customs in all three countries.

Considering your interests you enjoy history water activities and trying local cuisine.

- Interests: Thailand offers historical sites such as Ayutthaya and Sukhothai beautiful island destinations like Krabi and Phuket for water activities and diverse food experiences in Bangkok. Vietnam offers historical sites like Hoi An and Hue Halong Bay for a scenic cruise and popular dishes like pho and banh mi. Cambodia is known for Angkor Wat the awe-inspiring temple complex and offers unique Khmer cuisine.

- Budget: After reviewing the cost of accommodations transportation and meals in all three countries you find that Cambodia fits your budget the best followed by Thailand and Vietnam. You decide to spend more time in Cambodia to fully experience the culture and temples while allocating shorter durations for Thailand and Vietnam.

- Transportation: You research flights and find that there are direct flights to Bangkok from your home country making Thailand easily accessible. Vietnam and Cambodia have well-connected domestic flight networks making it convenient to travel between cities within each country.

- Accommodation: Thailand offers a wide range of accommodation options for all budgets including luxury resorts budget hostels and guesthouses. Vietnam also has a good variety of accommodations while Cambodia has a mix of luxury resorts and budget guesthouses with fewer mid-range options.

Determining the Length of Your Trip:

After considering your time constraints you have two weeks available for your trip.

- Prioritizing Destinations: You decide to spend the first week exploring the historical sites and enjoying water activities in Thailand. The second week will be divided between Vietnam and Cambodia with a few days in each country to visit the major attractions.

- Travel Pace: You prefer a relaxed travel pace allowing you to fully experience each destination. You allocate a minimum of three days in Thailand for exploring historic sites and three days in Cambodia for visiting Angkor Wat. The remaining days will be spent in Vietnam exploring popular destinations like Hoi An and Halong Bay.

- Travel Logistics: You allocate two days for travel between countries considering flight connections and travel time. This will give you ample time to explore each destination without feeling rushed.

By conducting thorough research considering your interests budget and time constraints you have successfully selected Thailand Vietnam and Cambodia as your destinations. You have also determined the length of your trip and allocated time for each country ensuring a well-rounded and exciting travel experience.

Chapter 2: Creating a Travel Budget

2.1 Assessing Your Financial Resources

When it comes to planning a trip the first step in creating a travel budget is assessing your financial resources. This involves taking a close look at your income savings and any other sources of funds that you have available for your trip.

To start review your monthly income and determine how much you can realistically set aside for your travel budget. This could be a percentage of your monthly income or a fixed amount that you can comfortably save each month leading up to your trip.

Next evaluate your savings and see if you have any funds that you can allocate towards your travel budget. If you have a specific goal in mind for your trip such as a luxury vacation or a backpacking adventure you may need to save a significant amount of money in advance.

Additionally consider any other potential sources of funds that you may have such as investments or credit card rewards. These can be valuable resources to tap into to help finance your trip.

Once you have a clear understanding of your financial resources you can move on to budgeting for specific aspects of your trip.

2.2 Budgeting for Transportation

Transportation costs are often a significant part of a travel budget particularly if you're planning to travel long distances or to multiple destinations. When budgeting for transportation there are several factors to consider:

Airfare: If you're planning to fly to your destination research different airlines and compare prices to find the best deals. Be flexible with your travel dates if possible as flying on weekdays or during off-peak seasons can often result in lower airfare.

Ground transportation: Depending on your destination you may need to budget for ground transportation such as train or bus tickets rental cars or taxis. Research the cost of these options in advance and factor them into your budget accordingly.

Local transportation: Once you arrive at your destination consider the cost of getting around within the city or country. This could include public transportation fares taxi rides or the cost of renting bicycles or scooters.

It's important to research and estimate these costs as accurately as possible. Look for online resources travel forums or consult with travel agents to get an idea of the typical transportation expenses for your chosen destination.

2.3 Allocating Funds for Accommodation

Accommodation expenses can vary greatly depending on your travel destination preferences and the level of comfort you're seeking. Here are a few considerations when budgeting for accommodation:

Hotel options: Research the range of hotels available in your destination from budget to luxury options. Compare prices read reviews and consider the location and amenities to find the best fit for your budget.

Alternative accommodations: Consider alternative options such as vacation rentals hostels or even staying with local residents through platforms like Airbnb or Couchsurfing. These options can often be more affordable and provide a unique experience.

Duration of stay: Take into account the number of nights you'll be staying. If you plan to travel for an extended period consider a mix of accommodations to suit your budget more effectively.

It's essential to include accommodation costs in your budget as it can significantly impact the overall cost of your trip. By carefully evaluating your preferences and weighing the options you can allocate the appropriate funds for your lodging needs.

2.4 Planning for Meals and Entertainment

Meals and entertainment expenses can also add up quickly while traveling. Here are some factors to consider when budgeting for these expenses:

Food options: Research the typical cost of meals at restaurants in your destination. Take note of the cost differences between local eateries and more upscale establishments. Additionally consider the option of cooking some meals for yourself if you have access to a kitchen in your accommodation.

Entertainment activities: Think about the activities you plan to enjoy while traveling such as museum visits tours or outdoor excursions. Research the cost of these activities in advance and allocate funds accordingly. Look for any discounts or special deals available as these can help you save money.

Budgeting for meals and entertainment can involve some flexibility and decision-making during your trip. You may choose to splurge on a few special meals or activities while being more frugal on other days. Remember to factor in these expenses when creating your travel budget to ensure you have funds available for memorable experiences.

2.5 Accounting for Miscellaneous Expenses

When creating a travel budget don't forget to account for miscellaneous expenses that may arise during your trip. These expenses can vary greatly and will depend on your destination travel style and personal preferences. Here are a few examples:

Visas and travel insurance: Some countries require visas for entry and travel insurance is highly recommended. Research the costs associated with these requirements and include them in your budget.

Souvenirs and shopping: If you plan on bringing back souvenirs or doing some shopping while traveling allocate funds to cover these expenses.

Emergency funds: It's always a good idea to have emergency funds set aside for unexpected situations such as medical emergencies or lost belongings.

Tips and gratuities: Depending on your destination tipping may be customary. Research the local customs and include an estimate of tipping expenses in your budget.

Communication costs: If you plan on using your mobile phone or accessing the internet while traveling research the potential costs for data roaming or purchasing local SIM cards.

By accounting for these miscellaneous expenses you'll have a more realistic view of the total cost of your trip. It's always better to overestimate your budget and have extra funds available should unexpected expenses arise.

In conclusion creating a travel budget involves assessing your financial resources budgeting for transportation allocating funds for accommodation planning for meals and entertainment and accounting for miscellaneous expenses. By carefully considering these aspects and conducting thorough research you can create a budget that allows you to enjoy your trip while staying within your financial means. Remember to be flexible and make adjustments as needed and always aim to set aside additional funds for unexpected expenses. With a well-planned travel budget you can embark on your journey with confidence and peace of mind.

Chapter 3: Planning your Itinerary

3.1 Defining Your Travel Goals

Before you start planning your itinerary it's important to define your travel goals. What are you hoping to achieve or experience during your trip? Are you looking to relax on a beach explore historical sites immerse yourself in a different culture try new adventurous activities or a combination of these? By setting clear travel goals you can tailor your itinerary to make the most of your time and ensure a fulfilling experience.

For example let's say your travel goal is to immerse yourself in a different culture. In this case you can prioritize visiting local markets attending cultural events or festivals exploring museums and interacting with the local community. On the other hand if your goal is to relax on a beach you would prioritize finding beachside accommodations including beach activities in your schedule and choosing destinations known for their beautiful beaches.

3.2 Mapping Out Your Route

Once you've defined your travel goals the next step is to map out your route. Start by identifying the destinations you want to visit and the order in which you plan to visit them. Look at a map or use travel planning websites or apps to get an idea of the distance and travel time between each destination.

Consider factors such as travel logistics including flight or train connections as well as visa requirements for each destination. It's essential to plan a route that makes logistical sense and takes into account any visa constraints or restrictions.

For example if you're planning a trip to Europe and want to visit multiple countries you could start by mapping out the major cities you want to visit such as Paris Rome and Barcelona. Consider the geographical proximity and choose a route that minimizes travel time and maximizes efficiency. This could mean starting in Paris taking a train to Rome and then flying to Barcelona.

3.3 Exploring Transportation Options

Once you have your route planned out it's time to consider your transportation options. Depending on your budget preferences and the location's infrastructure you can choose from various transportation modes such as flights trains buses rental cars or even walking and cycling.

Consider factors such as travel time cost convenience and sustainability when making transportation decisions. Research different airlines train companies and bus operators to find the best options for your itinerary. Additionally consider the local transportation options available at each destination to ensure smooth intra-city travel.

For example if you're planning a trip to Southeast Asia and want to explore multiple countries you can choose to fly between major cities to save time. On the other hand if you prefer a more immersive experience or have a limited budget you can opt for overland travel by taking trains buses or even hiring a private driver. This would allow you to experience the local culture and scenery along the way.

3.4 Allotting Time for Sightseeing and Activities

Once you have your travel logistics sorted it's crucial to plan the time you'll spend at each destination. Consider the duration of your trip and allocate an appropriate amount of time for each location based on your travel goals and the attractions or activities available.

Research the must-see sights or landmarks at each destination and prioritize them based on their significance and your interests. Take into account factors such as opening hours availability of guided tours and any seasonal or weather-related considerations. Also allow for some flexibility in your itinerary to accommodate unexpected discoveries or changes in plans.

For example if you're planning a trip to Japan and want to explore Tokyo Kyoto and Osaka you could allocate a few days to each city. In Tokyo you could visit popular attractions like the Tokyo Tower Shibuya Crossing and the Tsukiji Fish Market. In Kyoto you could dedicate time to visiting historic sites such as the Fushimi Inari Shrine and the Kinkaku-ji Temple. Finally in Osaka you could prioritize exploring the vibrant Dotonbori district and experiencing the local street food scene.

In conclusion planning your itinerary requires careful consideration of your travel goals mapping out your route exploring transportation options and allotting time for sightseeing and activities. By taking these steps and using examples to illustrate each point you can create a well-structured and enjoyable travel plan that maximizes your experience and ensures a memorable trip.

Chapter 4: Organizing your Travel Documents

4.1 Applying for Passports and Visas

One of the most important travel documents you will need is a passport. A passport is an official government document that serves as proof of identity and citizenship. It allows you to travel internationally and provides access to consular services while abroad. To apply for a passport you will need to visit your country's passport office or embassy and follow their application process.

The requirements for passport applications may vary from country to country but typically you will need to provide proof of citizenship (such as a birth certificate proof of identity (such as a driver's license a completed application form and passport-sized photos. You will also need to pay the applicable fees.

In addition to a passport you may also need a visa to enter certain countries. A visa is an official authorization that permits you to enter stay or transit through a foreign country for a specific period of time and purpose. Visa requirements vary depending on the country you wish to visit so it is important to research and understand the specific requirements for your destination.

To apply for a visa you will need to contact the embassy or consulate of the country you plan to visit. They will provide you with the necessary application forms and instructions. Visa applications often require you to provide documents such as a passport passport-sized photos a completed application form proof of accommodation and travel plans proof of financial means and an invitation letter (if applicable). It is recommended to start the visa application process well in advance of your travel dates as it can take some time to process.

Example:

Sarah is planning a trip to Italy. She is a United States citizen so she needs a passport to travel internationally. She goes to the passport office in her city and submits the required documents including her birth certificate driver's license completed application form and passport-sized photos. She pays the passport fee and is informed that her passport will be ready in approximately four weeks.

Sarah also learns that she needs a visa to enter Italy. She contacts the Italian embassy and receives the visa application forms. She gathers the necessary documents including her passport passport-sized photos completed application form proof of accommodation and travel plans proof of financial means and an invitation letter from a friend in Italy. Sarah submits her visa application well in advance of her trip to allow for processing time.

4.2 Ensuring Proper Identification and Copies

When traveling it is important to have proper identification readily available. In addition to your passport and visa you may need other forms of identification such as a driver's license or national identity card depending on your destination. Always check the entry requirements for the countries you plan to visit to ensure you have the necessary identification.

It is also recommended to carry multiple copies of your identification documents. Keep both physical and digital copies in separate locations. Physical copies can be stored in your luggage or a secure travel document organizer while digital copies can be stored on your smartphone or cloud storage. Having copies of your identification documents can be helpful in case your originals are lost or stolen during your trip.

Example:

John is traveling to Australia for a business conference. In addition to his passport and visa he knows that he may need to provide other forms of identification during his trip. He carries his valid driver's license as an additional form of identification.

To ensure the safety of his documents John makes multiple copies. He keeps one set of physical photocopies in his checked luggage and another set in a secure travel document organizer that he carries with him at all times. He also scans his passport visa and other identification documents and saves digital copies in his smartphone's storage and a cloud storage service.

4.3 Researching Entry and Exit Requirements

Entry and exit requirements can vary from country to country and can sometimes change with little notice. It is crucial to research and understand the specific entry and exit requirements for the countries you plan to visit.

Entry requirements usually include having a valid passport with a minimum validity period (often six months beyond your planned departure date a valid visa (if required and proof of sufficient funds for your stay. Some countries may also require proof of a return ticket or onward travel proof of accommodation or a vaccination certificate. It is important to check if you meet these requirements before embarking on your trip.

Exit requirements may include paying departure taxes or complying with specific customs regulations. Some countries may have restrictions on the amount of currency you can take out of the country or may require you to declare certain items. Familiarize yourself with the exit requirements of your destination to ensure a smooth departure.

Example:

Emily and James are planning a trip to Thailand. They research the entry requirements for Thai tourists and find that they will need a valid passport with at least six months validity a visa exemption or a tourist visa (depending on their nationality proof of a return ticket or onward travel and proof of sufficient funds for their stay.

Since they plan to travel around Thailand they also research the exit requirements and learn that they will need to pay a departure tax at the airport when leaving the country. Additionally they discover that there are restrictions on the amount of Thai currency they can take out of the country and that certain items such as Buddha images require special permits. Emily and James make notes of these requirements to ensure they comply with them during their trip.

4.4 Gathering Travel Insurances and Vaccination Certificates

Travel insurance is an essential document that provides financial protection in case of unexpected events or emergencies during your trip. It typically covers medical expenses trip cancellations or interruptions lost or delayed baggage and other related expenses. Before you travel it is wise to review different travel insurance options to find a policy that suits your needs.

Medical travel insurance is particularly important as it covers medical expenses in case of illness or injury while abroad. This is especially crucial if you are traveling to a country with high healthcare costs or limited access to medical facilities. Make sure to carefully review the coverage and limitations of your travel insurance policy to ensure it meets your specific needs.

In some cases you may also need to provide proof of certain vaccinations or carry an International Certificate of Vaccination or Prophylaxis (ICVP). Certain countries have strict entry requirements regarding vaccinations especially for diseases such as yellow fever or polio. Check the vaccination requirements for your destination well in advance and consult with a healthcare professional or travel clinic to ensure you are up to date on necessary vaccinations.

Example:

David is planning a backpacking trip across Southeast Asia. He knows that accidents or illnesses can happen so he decides to purchase travel insurance. He researches different insurance providers and chooses a policy that covers medical expenses trip cancellations and lost baggage.

Before his trip David visits a travel clinic to get the necessary vaccinations. The healthcare professional advises him to get vaccinations for hepatitis A typhoid and Japanese encephalitis as these diseases are prevalent in the region. David receives the vaccinations and gets an International Certificate of Vaccination as proof.

4.5 Keeping Digital Copies of Important Documents

In the digital age it is becoming increasingly important to keep digital copies of your important travel documents. This provides an additional layer of security and convenience as you can access your documents from anywhere with an internet connection.

Scan or take clear photos of your passport visa identification cards travel insurance policy vaccination certificates and any other important documents. Save these digital copies in a secure location such as an encrypted cloud storage service or a password-protected folder on your computer or smartphone. It is also a good idea to email the digital copies to yourself or a trusted friend or family member so you can access them in case your devices are lost stolen or damaged.

Having digital copies of your documents can be beneficial in various situations. For example if your passport is stolen you can show a digital copy to your country's embassy or consulate to start the process of obtaining a new one. Similarly if you need to provide proof of your travel insurance vaccination status or visa while abroad you can easily access the digital copies on your smartphone.

Example:

Maria is going on a backpacking trip through Europe. She knows that carrying physical copies of her important documents can be risky so she decides to create digital copies as well. She scans her passport visa and other documents and saves them in a password-protected folder on her laptop. She also uploads the files to a secure cloud storage service ensuring she can access them from any device with an internet connection.

During her trip Maria's backpack is stolen including her physical passport and identification cards. She immediately contacts the local authorities and then retrieves her digital copies from her cloud storage. She visits the nearest embassy and shows them the digital copies helping to expedite the process of obtaining a new passport.

In conclusion organizing your travel documents is a crucial step in ensuring a smooth and hassle-free trip. Applying for passports and visas ensuring proper identification and copies researching entry and exit requirements gathering travel insurances and vaccination certificates and keeping digital copies of important documents are all essential for a successful journey. By being well-prepared and organized you can minimize potential issues and enjoy your travels with peace of mind.

Chapter 5: Accommodation and Transportation

5.1 Choosing Accommodation Types

When traveling one of the most crucial decisions to make is choosing the right accommodation. There are various types of accommodations available ranging from hotels and hostels to vacation rentals and alternative options like couchsurfing. It is essential to consider your budget preferences and travel style when selecting the type of accommodation that suits you best.

Hotels: Hotels are the most common and widely available accommodation option. They offer a range of amenities services and room types catering to different budgets and preferences. From luxury five-star hotels to budget-friendly options hotels provide comfort convenience and professional service. They often include services like housekeeping room service and access to facilities such as swimming pools gyms and restaurants.

Example: Imagine you're planning a relaxing beach vacation. You want a luxury experience with a breathtaking view of the ocean. In this case choosing a five-star beachfront hotel with a spa gourmet restaurant and private beach access would be an excellent option.

Hostels: Hostels are an affordable accommodation choice particularly popular among backpackers solo travelers and those seeking a social atmosphere. Hostels generally offer shared dormitory-style rooms with bunk beds as well as private rooms at a higher cost. Common areas such as lounges and kitchens encourage interaction between guests fostering a vibrant community of international travelers.

Example: Suppose you're exploring a vibrant city known for its nightlife and cultural attractions. You're traveling on a tight budget and enjoy meeting new people. Opting for a centrally located hostel with a lively bar and common areas would suit your needs enabling you to socialize with fellow travelers and make new friends.

Vacation Rentals: Vacation rentals provide an alternative to traditional accommodations. They range from apartments and houses to villas offering the comforts of a home away from home. Vacation rentals are ideal for families or groups as they often include multiple bedrooms a kitchen and common areas. Booking a vacation rental can offer privacy flexibility and the opportunity to immerse yourself in the local culture.

Example: Suppose you're traveling with your extended family for a week-long vacation. Renting a spacious beachfront villa with multiple bedrooms a fully equipped kitchen and a private pool would allow everyone to stay together comfortably and create lasting memories.

5.2 Booking Hotels Hostels or Vacation Rentals

Once you have determined the type of accommodation that suits your needs the next step is booking your desired stay. There are several options available for booking accommodations depending on your preferred method and convenience.

Online Travel Agencies (OTAs): Online travel agencies such as Expedia Booking.com and Airbnb have made booking accommodations simple and convenient. These platforms offer a wide range of choices with detailed descriptions photos reviews and competitive pricing. They allow you to browse and compare various accommodation options and book directly through their websites or mobile apps.

Example: Utilizing an online travel agency you can search for hotels hostels or vacation rentals in your desired location select specific criteria such as price range amenities and guest ratings to narrow down your options. Once you find a suitable accommodation you can secure your reservation with a few clicks and receive a confirmation email.

Direct Booking: Some accommodations provide the option to book directly through their own websites or by contacting them directly via phone or email. Booking directly with the establishment can sometimes offer additional benefits such as better rates loyalty program rewards or personalized services.

Example: Suppose you have a preferred hotel chain and are

a member of their loyalty program. Directly booking a room through their website allows you to take advantage of exclusive discounts and earn loyalty points for future stays.

Travel Agents: If you prefer personalized assistance and guidance working with a travel agent can be an option. Travel agents have expertise in finding suitable accommodations based on your preferences budget and specific needs. They can also provide additional services such as arranging transportation and booking tours.

Example: If you're planning a luxury honeymoon a travel agent can help you select and book a romantic suite in a boutique hotel ensuring a memorable and intimate getaway experience.

5.3 Exploring Alternate Accommodation Options

In addition to traditional accommodations there are alternative options available that offer unique experiences and opportunities for cultural immersion.

Couchsurfing: Couchsurfing is a platform that connects travelers with local hosts who offer a spare couch or room for free. It provides an excellent opportunity to stay with locals experience their culture firsthand and make meaningful connections. Couchsurfing relies on trust and mutual respect between guests and hosts.

Example: Imagine you're traveling to a foreign country where you want to learn more about the local customs and traditions. By couchsurfing with a local host you can gain insights into their way of life try authentic local cuisine and participate in cultural activities.

House Sitting: House sitting involves taking care of someone else's property pets or plants while they are away in exchange for accommodation. Various online platforms connect homeowners with house sitters allowing travelers to stay in a local home for free or at a significantly reduced rate.

Example: If you're an animal lover and enjoy the comforts of a home environment house sitting can be an appealing option. You could take care of a homeowner's pets while they're traveling and have the opportunity to explore a new city or country without the cost of accommodation.

5.4 Comparing Transportation Modes

Once you have sorted out your accommodation the next aspect to consider is transportation. Choosing the right transportation mode depends on factors such as destination budget travel duration and personal preferences.

Air Travel: Air travel is the fastest and most convenient way to cover long distances. It allows you to reach your destination quickly making it suitable for international or intercontinental travel. Airlines offer various fare classes from economy to business or first class providing different levels of comfort services and amenities.

Example: If you're traveling from New York to Tokyo flying would be the most time-efficient option allowing you to reach your destination in around 14 hours. You can choose a comfortable seat enjoy in-flight entertainment and have meals served during the journey.

Train Travel: Train travel is an excellent option for both short and medium distances especially within a country or continental region. Trains offer the advantage of scenic routes larger legroom compared to planes and the ability to move around during the journey. Some trains even provide sleeper compartments for overnight travel.

Example: Suppose you're exploring Europe and want to travel from Paris to Amsterdam. Taking a high-speed train like the Thalys would allow you to enjoy the picturesque countryside views relax in spacious seats and have access to onboard amenities like food and wifi.

Bus Travel: Buses are a cost-effective means of transportation particularly for shorter distances or within a specific region. They offer frequent departures flexibility in choosing departure and arrival locations and generally have lower fares compared to other modes of transport. Some buses provide additional amenities like onboard restrooms and entertainment systems.

Example: If you're traveling from Edinburgh to Glasgow in Scotland taking a bus would be a convenient option. Buses run frequently between the cities offering a comfortable ride and the opportunity to admire the Scottish landscapes along the way.

Car Rental: Renting a car gives you complete freedom and flexibility while traveling. It allows you to explore off-the-beaten-path destinations create your itinerary and travel at your own pace. Car rentals are particularly advantageous if you're traveling with a group carrying heavy luggage or visiting remote areas with limited public transportation.

Example: Suppose you're planning a road trip along the California coastline starting in San Francisco and ending in Los Angeles. Renting a car would enable you to stop at scenic viewpoints explore national parks and take detours to charming coastal towns along the way.

5.5 Evaluating Pros and Cons of Public Transport and Rental Vehicles

When deciding between public transport and rental vehicles it is crucial to evaluate the pros and cons of each option based on your specific travel needs.

Public Transport:

- Pros: Public transport systems such as trains buses and subways are often well-developed in cities and tourist destinations offering extensive coverage and frequent schedules. They are cost-effective environmentally friendly and allow you to immerse yourself in the local culture by interacting with locals and fellow passengers. Public transport is often reliable saving you the hassle of navigating unfamiliar roads or dealing with parking.
- Cons: Depending on the destination public transport can be crowded especially during peak hours and may have limited schedules or routes. It can be less convenient for carrying large luggage or traveling with young children. Public transport also

requires careful planning to ensure you reach your destination on time and may involve transfers or walking distances.

Example: If you're visiting London public transport in the form of the Underground (Tube) system is an excellent option. It covers the entire city operates frequently and bypasses traffic congestion. You can save money by purchasing a travelcard or using contactless payment options like Oyster cards to enjoy unlimited rides.

Rental Vehicles:
- Pros: Rental vehicles provide flexibility allowing you to explore remote areas follow your own schedule and carry bulky luggage. They are convenient for families or groups as everyone can travel together in one vehicle. Rental vehicles also offer privacy comfort and the ability to customize your travel experience such as choosing the music or making stops whenever you wish.
- Cons: Renting a vehicle involves additional costs such as rental fees insurance fuel and parking fees. It requires driving skills a valid driver's license and familiarity with local traffic rules and road conditions. In congested cities finding affordable parking and dealing with traffic can be challenging and time-consuming.

Example: If you're planning a countryside exploration of Tuscany renting a car would allow you to visit charming villages vineyards and remote landscapes at your own pace. You can experience the freedom of stopping wherever you please to capture beautiful views or indulge in local cuisine.

In conclusion selecting the right accommodation and transportation options can significantly impact your travel experience. Consider your budget preferences travel style and specific needs when choosing accommodations such as hotels hostels vacation rentals or alternative options like couchsurfing and house sitting. Assessing the pros and cons of transportation modes like air travel train travel bus travel and car rental will help you make informed decisions about the most suitable mode for your journey. Whether you opt for public transport or rental vehicles each option has its advantages and considerations to ensure a smooth and enjoyable trip.

Chapter 6: Staying Safe and Healthy

6.1 Familiarizing with Local Laws and Customs

When traveling to a new destination it is important to familiarize yourself with the local laws and customs to ensure a safe and enjoyable trip. Each country has its own set of rules and regulations and being aware of them can help you avoid potentially harmful situations or legal trouble.

Start by researching the basic laws of the country you're visiting. This includes understanding the legal drinking age smoking regulations and drug laws. In some countries certain medications that are legal in your home country may be prohibited so it's crucial to check the specific guidelines.

Additionally learn about the cultural norms and customs of the destination. This can help you avoid inadvertently offending locals or engaging in inappropriate behavior. For example in some countries it may be considered disrespectful to wear revealing clothing or to display public affection.

It's also worth researching any local scams or tourist-targeted crimes that may be prevalent in the area. Knowing what to expect and how to prevent falling victim to these scams can greatly enhance your safety while traveling.

6.2 Basic Travel Safety Tips

Traveling can be exciting but it's important to prioritize your safety throughout your trip. Here are some basic travel safety tips to keep in mind:

1. Stay aware of your surroundings: Pay attention to your environment and be cautious of any suspicious individuals or activities. If something doesn't feel right trust your instincts and remove yourself from the situation.

2. Secure your belongings: Keep your personal belongings secure especially in crowded areas or public transportation. Use locks on your luggage and consider investing in a money belt to keep your valuables safe.

3. Stay in touch with loved ones: Share your travel plans with trusted friends or family members and keep them updated on your whereabouts. This way someone will know where you are in case of an emergency.

4. Use reputable transportation: When using public transportation or hiring a taxi choose reputable services and drivers. Avoid unmarked vehicles or unlicensed operators.

5. Use hotel safes: Store your important documents extra cash

and valuable items in the hotel safe whenever possible. This provides an extra layer of security for your belongings.

6. Keep copies of important documents: Make copies or take photos of your passport visas and other important documents. This can be helpful in case your originals are lost or stolen.

7. Be cautious with public Wi-Fi: Public Wi-Fi networks can be insecure so avoid accessing sensitive information such as online banking or entering passwords while connected to these networks. Consider using a virtual private network (VPN) to encrypt your internet connection.

6.3 Handling Emergency Situations

While we hope you never find yourself in an emergency situation while traveling it's important to know how to handle them if they arise. Here are some steps to take in various emergency scenarios:

1. Medical emergencies: If you or someone with you requires immediate medical attention call the local emergency services right away. It's also a good idea to have travel insurance that covers medical expenses so you can receive the necessary care without financial burden.

2. Natural disasters: If you're traveling to an area prone to natural disasters such as hurricanes or earthquakes familiarize yourself with the local evacuation procedures. Stay informed through official sources and follow instructions given by local authorities.

3. Theft or loss of belongings: If you're a victim of theft or lose your belongings report the incident to the local police as soon as possible. Contact your travel insurance provider to understand the process for filing a claim.

4. Consular assistance: If you find yourself in a situation where you require assistance from your country's consulate or embassy contact them immediately. They can provide guidance and support especially in cases involving legal issues or loss of travel documents.

6.4 Staying Healthy on the Road

Maintaining good health while traveling is essential in order to make the most of your trip. Here are some tips for staying healthy:

1. Stay hydrated: Drink plenty of water especially in hot climates or during physical activities. Carry a reusable water bottle and refill it regularly.

2. Practice good hygiene: Regularly wash your hands with soap and water or use hand sanitizers when soap is not available. This is particularly important before eating or touching your face to prevent the spread of germs.

3. Eat well-balanced meals: Aim to include a variety of fruits vegetables lean proteins and whole grains in your diet. Be cautious when consuming street food and choose food from reputable establishments to minimize the risk of foodborne illnesses.

4. Get enough sleep: Adequate sleep is crucial for maintaining good health and energy levels. Try to establish a sleep routine that allows for sufficient rest even while adjusting to different time zones.

5. Practice safe sex: If you engage in sexual activity while traveling ensure that you practice safe sex to prevent the transmission of sexually transmitted infections.

6. Protect yourself from insect bites: In areas where insect-borne diseases are prevalent use insect repellent and wear appropriate clothing to protect yourself from mosquito bites.

7. Stay active: Incorporate physical activity into your travel itinerary. It could be walking tours hiking swimming or any other form of exercise that you enjoy. Staying active helps boost your energy levels and enhances your overall well-being.

6.5 Managing Medications and Vaccinations

If you take prescription medications it's important to plan ahead to ensure you have an adequate supply while traveling. Here are some tips for managing medications:

1. Carry prescriptions and medical information: Keep a copy of your prescriptions including generic names in case you need to refill your medications abroad. It's also helpful to carry a letter from your healthcare provider explaining your medical condition and the necessity of the medications.

2. Pack medications in your carry-on: Always keep your

medications as well as any necessary medical supplies in your carry-on luggage. This will ensure you have access to them in case your checked luggage is lost or delayed.

3. Research local regulations: Understand the regulations surrounding the importation of medications in the country you're visiting. Some countries may have restrictions or require specific documentation for certain medications.

4. Plan for vaccinations: Depending on your destination you may need certain vaccinations or booster shots. Consult with a healthcare professional or a travel clinic well in advance to ensure you have all the necessary vaccinations before your trip.

5. Consider travel insurance: Look into travel insurance that covers medical emergencies and the cost of medications. This can provide peace of mind and financial protection in case of unforeseen medical expenses.

In conclusion staying safe and healthy while traveling is crucial for an enjoyable trip. By familiarizing yourself with local laws and customs following basic travel safety tips knowing how to handle emergency situations practicing good health habits and managing medications and vaccinations you can enhance your overall travel experience and minimize potential risks. Remember to plan ahead stay informed and prioritize your well-being throughout your journey.

Chapter 7: Immersing in the Local Culture

7.1 Learning Basic Phrases and Customs:

One of the most important aspects of immersing oneself in a local culture is learning the basic language and customs of the region. By being able to communicate with locals in their own language you can build connections and gain a deeper understanding of their culture. Additionally understanding local customs will help you navigate social situations with ease and show respect to the locals.

When learning basic phrases it's essential to focus on greetings common expressions and simple conversational phrases. For example in Japan it is customary to greet someone with a bow instead of a handshake. Learning how to say "hello" (konnichiwa "thank you" (arigatou gozaimasu and "excuse me" (sumimasen) in Japanese would be invaluable in communicating with locals.

In some cultures it is customary to use honorifics or titles when addressing someone. In Korea for instance it is respectful to address someone older or with a higher social status using honorifics like "oppa" (for older brother) or "sunbae" (for someone senior in school or work). Learning these nuances and using them in appropriate situations can greatly enhance your interactions with locals.

It's important to note that while learning basic phrases can be helpful it's equally crucial to practice pronunciation and intonation. This will not only help you be understood but also make it easier for locals to engage with you.

7.2 Seeking Authentic Local Experiences:

To truly immerse yourself in a local culture it's important to go beyond tourist attractions and seek out authentic experiences. This can involve exploring local neighborhoods visiting traditional markets or engaging with local artisans and craftsmen.

For example if you're visiting Thailand instead of sticking to the popular tourist spots in cities like Bangkok or Phuket you can venture into smaller towns and villages to experience the local way of life. You could visit a floating market where locals sell fresh produce and handicrafts from their boats or participate in a traditional Thai cooking class to learn about the ingredients and techniques used in their cuisine.

In India attending a traditional wedding ceremony can provide a rich cultural experience. From vibrant celebrations to intricate rituals a traditional wedding showcases various customs and traditions that are deeply ingrained in Indian culture. By being respectful and observing the customs you can gain insights into the local way of life.

By seeking out these authentic experiences you not only get a chance to witness the local culture firsthand but also support local businesses and artisans. It is a win-win situation where you can learn connect and contribute to the local community.

7.3 Discovering Traditional Cuisine:

Food is an integral part of any culture and exploring traditional cuisine is a fantastic way to immerse yourself in the local way of life. Every region has its unique flavors ingredients and cooking techniques that reflect its history climate and available resources.

For instance in Mexico you can indulge in dishes like tacos enchiladas and guacamole which give insights into the country's rich culinary heritage. Trying local street food such as tamales or elote (grilled corn can be a delicious and immersive culinary experience.

Similarly in Italy you can explore regional specialties like pasta pizza and gelato. Each region has its variations and traditional recipes that have been passed down through generations. By trying these dishes you not only satisfy your taste buds but also gain a deeper appreciation for the local culture and its culinary traditions.

A great way to further enhance your understanding of local cuisine is by taking cooking classes or visiting local food markets. In Thailand for example you can join a cooking class to learn how to prepare traditional dishes like pad thai or green curry. These experiences not only teach you cooking techniques but also provide insights into the cultural significance of certain ingredients and cooking methods.

7.4 Understanding Local Etiquette:

Every culture has its unique set of social norms and etiquette and understanding and respecting these customs can make a significant difference in your interactions with locals. By familiarizing yourself with local etiquette you can avoid unintentionally offending or misunderstanding others.

For example in many Asian cultures it is considered impolite to touch someone's head as the head is considered sacred. In Thailand you should avoid pointing your feet at people or sacred objects as feet are considered the lowest and dirtiest part of the body. By being aware of these customs you can show respect and avoid any unintentional offense.

Additionally understanding concepts of personal space and appropriate gestures is essential. In some cultures like Japan there is a greater emphasis on personal space and physical contact may be kept at a minimum. Being aware of these cultural differences allows you to adapt your behavior and communicate effectively without causing discomfort.

Furthermore respecting local customs regarding dress code is crucial. For example in many religious sites visitors are required to dress modestly and cover their shoulders and knees. By following these guidelines you can show respect for the local culture and traditions.

7.5 Participating in Cultural Festivals and Events:

Attending cultural festivals and events is a fantastic way to immerse yourself in the local culture and witness its vibrant traditions and celebrations. Festivals provide insight into a culture's history beliefs and values while offering a unique opportunity to engage with locals and understand their way of life.

For example in Brazil the annual Carnival festival is a world-renowned celebration of music dance and vibrant costumes. By attending this festival you can experience the energy and joy of Brazilian culture and witness the Samba dancing and music that are deeply rooted in the country's history.

In India festivals like Diwali (Festival of Lights Holi (Festival of Colors and Navaratri (Nine-Night Festival) offer a glimpse into the country's rich cultural and religious traditions. From lighting lamps and bursting fireworks to playing with colored powders and dancing to traditional music these festivals provide a visual and sensory extravaganza.

Participating in these festivals allows you to engage with locals learn about their customs and even participate in the festivities. Whether it's joining a procession trying traditional costumes or learning traditional dances these experiences can create lasting memories and deepen your connection with the local culture.

In conclusion immersing yourself in the local culture involves learning basic phrases and customs seeking authentic experiences discovering traditional cuisine understanding local etiquette and participating in cultural festivals and events. By embracing these aspects you can gain a deeper understanding of the local way of life build meaningful connections with locals and create enriching experiences that go beyond the surface-level tourist experiences. So when traveling or living abroad make a conscious effort to engage with the local culture and make the most of your experiences.

Chapter 8: Budget-Friendly Sightseeing and Activities

8.1 Finding Free or Low-Cost Attractions

When travelling on a budget one of the best ways to save money is by exploring free or low-cost attractions. These attractions may not be as well-known or popular as their expensive counterparts but they can still offer memorable experiences and insights into the local culture. Here are some strategies for finding these budget-friendly attractions:

1. Research online: Before you travel conduct thorough research online to discover free or low-cost attractions in your destination. Many travel websites blogs and forums provide valuable information on off-the-beaten-path attractions that won't break the bank.

2. Visit local tourism offices: Tourism offices are a great resource for finding budget-friendly attractions. They often have brochures and maps that highlight free or low-cost activities in the area. The staff can also provide recommendations based on your interests and budget.

3. Utilize travel apps: There are numerous travel apps available that specialize in finding budget-friendly attractions. These apps often include user reviews maps and detailed information about free or low-cost sights and activities. Some popular apps include TripAdvisor Yelp and Lonely Planet.

4. Take advantage of city passes: Many major cities offer city passes or tourist cards that provide discounts on attractions public transportation and even dining options. These passes can save you a significant amount of money if you plan to visit multiple paid attractions.

Example: Let's say you're visiting New York City on a budget. By researching online you discover that the Staten Island Ferry offers free rides and provides stunning views of the Statue of Liberty and the Manhattan skyline. Additionally you find out that many museums and attractions in the city offer free admission on certain days or during specific hours. By planning your itinerary accordingly you can save a substantial amount of money while still enjoying the city's popular attractions.

8.2 Taking Advantage of Local Deals and Discounts

In addition to free or low-cost attractions there are often local deals and discounts available that can help you save money on sightseeing and activities. Here are some strategies for finding and taking advantage of these deals:

1. Check local coupon books and magazines: Many cities have coupon books or magazines that offer discounts on attractions restaurants and other services. These publications are often

available at tourism offices hotels or even online.

2. Follow local social media accounts: Many cities and attractions have social media accounts where they post updates promotions and exclusive discounts. By following these accounts you can stay up-to-date on the latest deals and take advantage of them before they expire.

3. Look for package deals: Sometimes attractions and activities offer package deals that include multiple experiences at a discounted price. These can be a great way to save money while enjoying a variety of activities. For example a package deal might include admission to a museum a guided tour and a meal at a discounted rate.

Example: Let's say you're travelling to London and want to visit multiple paid attractions. You find a deal online that offers discounted combined tickets for popular attractions like the Tower of London the London Eye and the Madame Tussauds wax museum. By purchasing the combined ticket you save a significant amount of money compared to buying individual tickets for each attraction.

8.3 Exploring Outdoor Activities and Nature Sites

Nature sites and outdoor activities often provide budget-friendly alternatives to expensive tourist attractions. These activities not only offer unique experiences but also allow you to connect with nature and enjoy the beauty of your destination. Here are some outdoor activities and nature sites to consider:

1. Hiking and walking trails: Many destinations have scenic hiking and walking trails that are free to use. These trails can lead you to breathtaking views waterfalls natural landmarks and wildlife. Always check local regulations and safety guidelines before embarking on any hiking or walking adventure.

2. Beaches and parks: Beaches and parks are often free or have a minimal entrance fee. They provide opportunities for swimming sunbathing picnicking and enjoying outdoor recreational activities. These natural settings can be perfect for relaxing and unwinding without spending a lot of money.

3. Wildlife spotting: If you're interested in observing wildlife consider visiting national parks reserves or wildlife sanctuaries. These natural habitats allow you to see a variety of species in their natural environment. Some destinations even offer guided tours led by experienced naturalists to enhance your wildlife spotting experience.

Example: Suppose you're travelling to Thailand and want to experience its natural beauty without breaking the bank. You discover that the Khao Sok National Park offers hiking trails kayaking and wildlife spotting opportunities at a reasonable cost. By immersing yourself in the stunning rainforest you can see diverse flora and fauna visit the iconic Cheow Lan Lake and maybe even spot some rare animals like elephants tigers or gibbons.

8.4 Engaging in Community-Based Tourism

Another budget-friendly option is to engage in community-based tourism. Community-based tourism focuses on visiting local communities interacting with residents and learning about their culture and way of life. These experiences are often more authentic and immersive than mainstream tourist activities and they usually come at a lower cost. Here's how you can engage in community-based tourism:

1. Homestays: Consider staying with local families or in guesthouses run by community members. This provides an opportunity to experience daily life eat local cuisine and learn about the traditions and customs of the host community. Homestays are often more affordable than hotels and offer a unique cultural exchange.

2. Participate in cultural activities: Many communities organize cultural activities such as traditional dances cooking classes handicraft workshops or farming experiences. These activities not only give you a deeper understanding of the local culture but also provide income and support to the community members.

3. Volunteer: Some destinations offer volunteer opportunities where you can contribute to community development projects. This could involve assisting with education conservation healthcare or infrastructure improvement initiatives. Volunteering allows you to give back while experiencing the local culture and forming meaningful connections.

Example: Suppose you're visiting Peru and want to immerse yourself in the indigenous culture of the Andean communities. You find a community-based tourism organization that offers homestays in small villages like Cusco or Puno. During your stay you have the chance to participate in traditional ceremonies learn about local weaving techniques and even help with farming activities. Not only do you get an authentic cultural experience but you also support the local economy and contribute to the community's well-being.

8.5 Supporting Sustainable Tourism Initiatives

Lastly supporting sustainable tourism initiatives can be a great way to engage in budget-friendly sightseeing and activities. Sustainable tourism focuses on minimizing negative environmental social and cultural impacts while maximizing positive contributions to the destination. Here are some ways you can support sustainable tourism:

1. Use public transportation: Instead of relying on taxis or rental cars try using public transportation like buses trains or bicycles. Not only is this more affordable but it also reduces carbon emissions and traffic congestion contributing to a more sustainable environment.

2. Eat at locally-owned restaurants and markets: Supporting local restaurants and markets helps to boost the local economy and preserve culinary traditions. These establishments often use locally-sourced ingredients reducing the carbon footprint of your meals. Additionally eating at local eateries tends to be more budget-friendly than dining at tourist-centric restaurants.

3. Choose eco-friendly accommodations: Look for accommodations that have environmentally sustainable practices such as energy-efficient buildings recycling programs and sustainable

water and waste management. Some accommodations even have initiatives to support local communities or conservation projects.

Example: Let's say you're visiting Costa Rica known for its commitment to sustainable tourism. You choose to stay at an eco-lodge that uses renewable energy promotes responsible waste management and supports local conservation projects. The lodge offers hiking trails on its premises allowing you to explore the surrounding nature without additional costs. By choosing sustainable accommodations and activities you not only enjoy your travels but also contribute to the preservation of Costa Rica's natural beauty.

In conclusion finding budget-friendly sightseeing and activities requires a little bit of research creativity and flexibility. By seeking out free or low-cost attractions taking advantage of local deals and discounts exploring outdoor activities and nature sites engaging in community-based tourism and supporting sustainable tourism initiatives you can have a fulfilling travel experience without breaking the bank. Remember the goal is not just to save money but also to create meaningful connections learn about different cultures and contribute positively to the destinations you visit.

Important Tips

Here are 100 amazing trip tips to enhance your travel experience:

1. Research your destination thoroughly before you go.
2. Create a travel itinerary including must-see attractions and activities.
3. Pack light and efficiently including only the essentials.
4. Bring a reusable water bottle to stay hydrated on the go.
5. Keep an emergency kit with basic first aid supplies.
6. Learn a few basic phrases in the local language.
7. Carry a power bank for charging your devices on the move.
8. Use a money belt or hidden pouch to keep your valuables safe.
9. Familiarize yourself with the local customs and etiquette.
10. Check the weather forecast for your destination beforehand.
11. Download offline maps or use a reliable GPS app on your phone.
12. Dress appropriately for the culture and climate of your destination.
13. Support local businesses and try authentic local cuisine.
14. Try street food but be cautious about hygiene and safety.
15. Make copies of important travel documents and keep them

separately.

16. Stay connected with loved ones by sharing your travel updates.

17. Take photos but don't forget to live in the moment and enjoy the experience.

18. Respect the environment by practicing sustainable tourism.

19. Carry a light rain jacket or poncho for unexpected showers.

20. Stay flexible with your plans to make room for spontaneous adventures.

21. Use public transportation to experience the local way of life.

22. Stay in a local homestay or B&B for a more authentic experience.

23. Get travel insurance to protect yourself from unforeseen circumstances.

24. Pack a scarf or sarong which can be used as a blanket cover-up or as a makeshift towel.

25. Pack a small portable speaker to enjoy music wherever you go.

26. Always carry some local currency for emergencies or small purchases.

27. Stay hydrated during flights by drinking plenty of water.

28. Avoid over-touristed areas and explore off-the-beaten-path destinations.

29. Be respectful and mindful of the local culture and customs.

30. Learn a few key words and phrases of the local language.

31. Carry a reusable shopping bag for groceries and souvenirs.

32. Support local artisans by purchasing handmade souvenirs.

33. Learn to haggle in local markets to get the best prices.

34. Stay vigilant and keep an eye on your belongings at all

times.

35. Explore the local cuisine by trying new dishes and flavors.

36. Engage with the locals and learn about their way of life.

37. Take a guided tour to gain deeper insights into the local history and culture.

38. Plan your activities around sunrise or sunset for stunning views.

39. Be open-minded and embrace new experiences and perspectives.

40. Get lost in the streets and discover hidden gems.

41. Pack a small umbrella for unexpected rain showers.

42. Stay hydrated by drinking plenty of water throughout the day.

43. Use sunscreen even on cloudy days to protect your skin from the sun.

44. Respect the local wildlife and natural surroundings.

45. Stay updated on local customs and laws to avoid any trouble.

46. Carry a universal adapter to charge your devices.

47. Stay in accommodations with good reviews and located in safe areas.

48. Take advantage of free walking tours to get oriented in a new city.

49. Research local festivals and events happening during your visit.

50. Learn basic greetings and pleasantries in the local language.

51. Opt for public transportation or walking instead of taxis for short distances.

52. Stay respectful when visiting religious sites or monuments.

53. Pack a small portable umbrella or rain poncho for unpredictable weather.

54. Bring a small first aid kit with essentials like band-aids medication etc.

55. Learn about local transportation options to get around efficiently.

56. Share your travel experiences through a travel blog or social media.

57. Keep an open mind and embrace cultural differences.

58. Be mindful of local customs and dress appropriately.

59. Carry a travel pillow and blanket for long flights or train rides.

60. Keep a travel journal to document your experiences and memories.

61. Get off the beaten path and explore lesser-known neighborhoods.

62. Stay connected with your loved ones through international calling apps.

63. Try local street food for an authentic culinary experience.

64. Pack a portable phone charger for emergencies.

65. Learn about the local currency and how to handle it.

66. Respect the environment by practicing responsible tourism.

67. Take a cooking class to learn to prepare local dishes.

68. Carry a small daypack for your essentials during daily excursions.

69. Stay aware of your surroundings and trust your instincts.

70. Pack a small foldable tote bag for carrying souvenirs or groceries.

71. Avoid overtouristed areas and explore local neighborhoods.

72. Research local customs and etiquette to avoid unintentional offense.

73. Carry extra batteries and memory cards for your camera.

74. Stay hydrated by drinking water regularly especially in warm climates.

75. Learn about the local transportation system and get a local transport card if available.

76. Take breaks and allow yourself time to rest and rejuvenate.

77. Use a travel app to find the best local restaurants and attractions.

78. Check if you need any vaccinations before traveling to certain destinations.

79. Respect local wildlife and don't engage in activities that harm them.

80. Carry a reusable shopping bag to avoid using plastic bags.

81. Learn basic phrases in the local language to communicate with locals.

82. Carry a small first aid kit with band-aids and basic medications.

83. Stay aware of local customs and traditions to show respect.

84. Always have a backup plan in case of changes or delays.

85. Pack a travel-sized umbrella for unexpected rain showers.

86. Stay connected with loved ones through phone calls or video chats.

87. Practice responsible tourism by minimizing waste and respecting the environment.

88. Carry a portable charger for your electronic devices.

89. Respect local customs and dress modestly in religious or conservative areas.

90. Pack a small lock for hostel or hotel lockers.

91. Take the time to learn about the local history and culture.

92. Manage your budget by keeping track of your expenses.

93. Try local transportation options like tuk-tuks or rickshaws.

94. Pack a small first aid kit with basic medications and band-aids.

95. Stay open-minded and embrace new experiences.

96. Visit local markets to immerse yourself in the local atmosphere.

97. Keep a copy of your travel insurance policy with you.

98. Stay hydrated by drinking plenty of water throughout the day.

99. Carry a reusable water bottle to reduce plastic waste.

100. Enjoy every moment and create lifelong memories!

These tips should help you have an amazing trip wherever you go. Happy travels!

9 788119 786572